S0-BNK-837

DISCARDED

Nature's Children

BEES

Elin Kelsey

 Grolier

FACTS IN BRIEF

Classification of the Honeybee
    Class: *Insectae* (insects)
    Order: *Hymenoptera* (insects with membranous wings)
    Family: *Apidae* (bee family)
    Genus: *Apis*
    Species: *Apis mellifera* (honey-carrying bee)

World distribution.   Honeybees live worldwide except in polar regions.

Habitat.   Honeybees live wherever flowers provide sufficent food.

Distinctive physical characteristics.   Thick round body with black and yellow stripes.

Habits.   Social insects living in large colonies. Well-established division of labor among workers, drones and queens. Use dances to communicate location of flowers. Aid in the pollination of flowers while looking for food. Ability to detect changes in weather through changes in air pressure.

Published originally as
"Getting to Know . . . Nature's Children."

This series is approved and recommended by the Federation of Ontario Naturalists.

This library reinforced edition is available exclusively from:

Grolier Educational Corporation
Sherman Turnpike, Danbury, Connecticut 06816

Copyright © 1986 by Grolier Limited. All rights reserved.

Contents

Bzzzz! A busy honeybee buzzes by you on its way through your garden. Did you know that without the labors of honeybees like this one there would not be any honey to spread on your toast in the morning?

The bees you may see in your garden are worker bees. They live in a hive which is a bit like a castle. Deep inside this castle lives its ruler, the queen bee. She is fed and guarded by thousands of female worker bees. Also living in the castle are the male bees, or drones.

There are more than 22 000 kinds of bees in the world, but only honeybees live in hives and produce large amounts of honey. Let's take a closer look at the hard-working honeybee and at life inside the hive.

Honeybees were not found in North America until the seventeenth century when settlers brought them.

Bumble bee

Honeybee

Bee Basics

Everyone knows what a honeybee looks like. Its thick, round body and yellow and black stripes make it easy to spot. Insect-eating animals quickly learn that those stripes can mean a painful sting. In fact, the bee's stripes are such a good "stay away" warning that a few non-stinging insects have copied the striped pattern. These copycats are mistaken for bees and left alone.

Like all insects, a bee has six legs and its body is made up of three parts. It has a round head, a middle section called a thorax and an egg-shaped section on the end called an abdomen. Bees do not have bones. Instead, they have a hard outer "skin," called an exoskeleton, that supports their bodies from the outside.

This Beefly looks dangerous thanks to its resemblance to the honeybee, but it couldn't sting even if it wanted to.

Sensitive Bee Senses

You find out about the world through your eyes, ears, nose and fingers. A honeybee gets its information about what is happening in the world through its eyes, feelers and body hairs.

The bee has two enormous eyes which cover the whole sides of its head. Each eye is divided into more than 4000 tiny parts. When you see a flower, you see a single picture. But a bee probably sees a flower made up of thousands of little squares. Look through a fine wire screen at something and you will get an idea of how a bee might see.

Bees cannot see the color red—to them it looks like black. However they can see other colors that you cannot, just as dogs can hear sounds that you cannot.

In addition to its two large eyes the honeybee has three smaller eyes on the top of its head. If you look carefully you can see one of them on this bee.

9

A bee does not use a nose to smell as you do. Instead it smells with a pair of long furry feelers called antennae. But these antennae do more than just smell. By sticking them into a jar of jam, a bee not only knows how the jam smells, but how it tastes and feels too.

Bees also sense things through their hair. Each hair on the bee's fuzzy coat is as sensitive as a cat's whisker. These sensitive hairs help the honeybee to sense what is going on around it, particularly things that it cannot see. If a strange air current tickles the body hairs, the bee buzzes off.

The honeybee's sensitive antennae are constantly at work smelling and tasting everything they contact.

Weather Sense

If you are planning a picnic, keep an eye out for bees. Lots of bees around means the weather will probably be fine for a picnic. If the bees have disappeared, think twice. You might be in for rain. But how do the bees know that? They know because they can detect changes in the air pressure. A sudden drop in air pressure tells the bees that rain is on the way, and they do not leave the hive.

Rain is not the only thing that keeps bees in their hive. If the temperature falls below 10 degrees Celsius (50 degrees Fahrenheit), you will never see any bees. It is simply too cold for them to fly.

Now you know where the expression a "hive of activity" comes from.

Cold-weather Clusters

Like all insects, bees cannot completely control their body temperature. When they are outside the temperature of their bodies is about as warm—or as cold—as the air around them. And the colder it gets, the more slowly they move. When it gets really cold they can barely move at all, let alone fly.

On cold days the bees huddle inside their hive. The ones on the cold outer edges of the hive try to force their way farther in to keep warm. Even when it is below freezing outside, bees can make their hive as warm as a summer afternoon by clustering in this way.

Flying Aces

Sometimes in the summer the hive gets too hot instead of too cold. Then the bees use their built-in air conditioners to cool down their home. They simply flap their wings!

Every bee has two sets of wings—a large strong pair in the front and a small round pair hooked to the front ones. The wings on the right side of a bee always work together as do those on the left. Each wing is as thin and clear as a piece of plastic wrap. They may look too frail to lift a bee into the air, but do not be fooled. A honeybee can perform a most impressive air show.

For instance, if a worker bee suddenly spots a tasty flower, it can turn in mid-air and dive in for a closer look. After hovering for a moment, it might zoom off and then up, perhaps as high as your bedroom ceiling before flying on. Most amazing of all, in the time it takes you to blink, a flying bee flaps its wings 250 times.

Opposite page:

A worker honeybee's powerful wings will carry her five kilometres (3 miles) in just 12 minutes.

Honeycomb Hives

Many bees are kept by beekeepers and "farmed" for their honey. The beekeeper provides sturdy wooden boxes for the bees to build their hive in. But wild honeybees must make their own homes. They build hives in the hole of a hollow tree or in a rock crevice by glueing together thousands upon thousands of tiny wax rooms called cells.

Believe it or not, all the wax used for building comes from the bees themselves. It is made in special glands under their abdomens. With their feet, they scoop tiny flakes of the wax into their mouths. Then, just as you would tackle a hard piece of bubble gum, the bees soften the wax by chewing it. When the wax is soft the bees make the six-sided wax cells.

Most of these cells will be used for raising young worker bees and storing food. Slightly larger cells are built for the drones. And long thin cells are built for the queen bees.

*Sometimes honeybees build their hives
in the open hanging from tree
branches.*

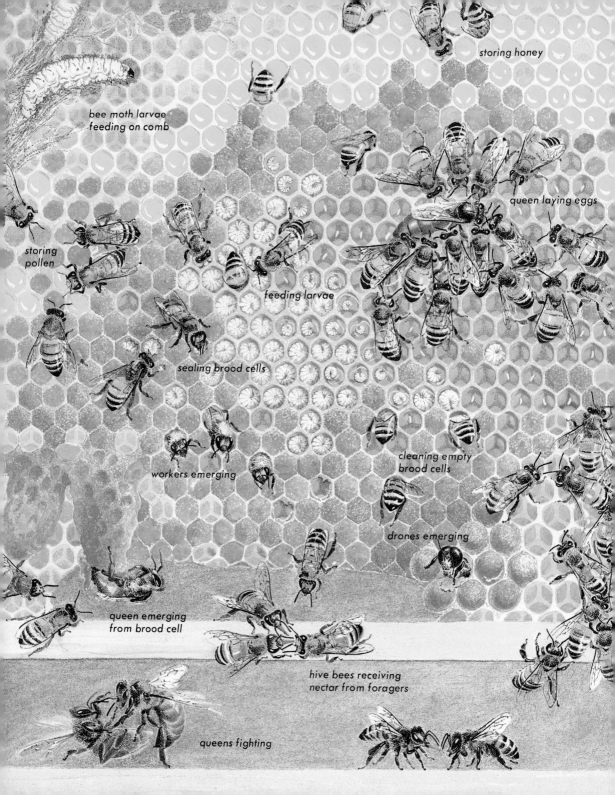

storing honey

bee moth larvae
feeding on comb

queen laying eggs

storing
pollen

feeding larvae

sealing brood cells

workers emerging

cleaning empty
brood cells

drones emerging

queen emerging
from brood cell

hive bees receiving
nectar from foragers

queens fighting

capping honey cells

scout performing
honey dance

building new
comb cells

ejecting drones

fanning and guarding
the hive entrance

Jobs for Everyone

Size comparison

Queen

Worker

Drone

All the hive-building work is done by the worker bees. And so is the housecleaning and food gathering. What then do the drones and the queen bee do?

The drone's job is to mate with the queen, and her job is to lay eggs so that there will always be new bees hatching. So, as you can see, each of the three types of honeybees has a special role in insuring the survival of the hive.

Both the queen and the drone are larger than the worker. The queen is the longest member of her colony. She is also the skinniest. The drone is fatter than the worker and the queen, and he has enormous eyes that cover most of the top of his head.

The queen and drone bees rarely leave the hive. When they do, they fly far higher than the worker bees, so we rarely see them.

The queen bee has been marked with a white spot. She will live about two or three years.

Moving Houses

A new hive is started when an older hive gets too large. Somehow the queen bee instinctively knows it is time for her to find new quarters. But before she leaves the old hive, she lays eggs in the long thin cells. These eggs are called royal eggs because they will grow into queen bees. These queen eggs are fed a special baby food called royal jelly.

When the new queens begin to hatch, the old queen can leave. She sends out scouts to find a new place for a hive. As soon as a good place is found, the old queen flies to it, followed by thousands of workers. This flying mass of bees is called a swarm. Bees usually swarm and build new hives in the spring.

A large swarm of honeybees may contain as many as 10 000 individuals!

Boscawen School Library
Merrimack Valley District

Queenly Duties

At the old hive, one new queen gets rid of all the others: there is only room for one queen in each hive. Then the new queen flies out, chased by the drones. The drones that catch and mate with her become the fathers of all the eggs that will be laid in the queen's lifetime.

A drone's life is easy, but it is also short. Soon after the queen has mated, the drones are turned away from the hive. Without the workers to feed them, the drones quickly die. However, the queen is treated royally when she returns to the hive. The workers pamper her and protect her as she begins to lay her eggs.

Amazing as it may seem, a queen can lay up to 1500 eggs in a single day. Over her lifetime, she may lay over one million eggs! She lays each of them in a special nursery cell and then has nothing more to do with them.

Royal cell-building.

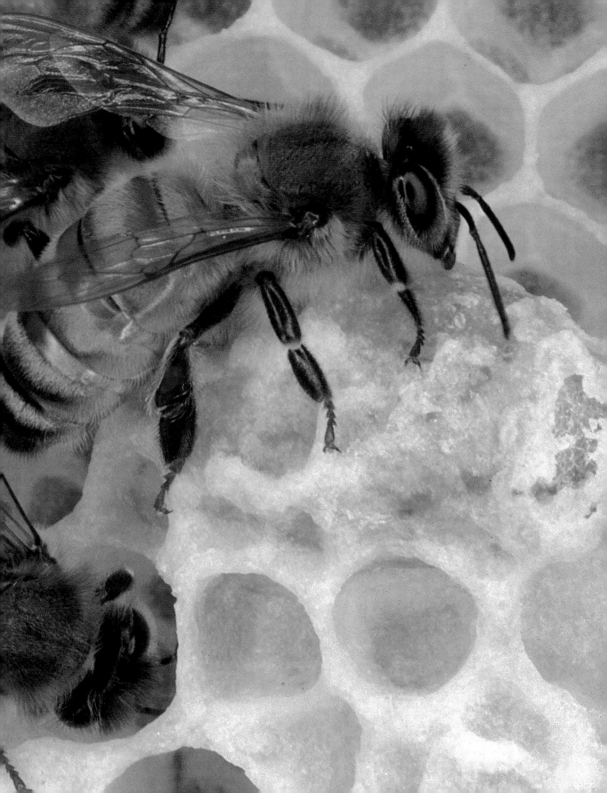

Baby Boomers

Bee eggs are so tiny that one of them could fit on the dot of this ''i.'' After just three days, a little white grub hatches out of each egg. These wormlike creatures do not look like adult bees—they do not have wings or legs or even proper heads.

The grubs are fed immediately by worker bees. They eat so much that they grow to adult size in just six days. Royal jelly is the secret to the grubs' amazing growth. Queen grubs eat royal jelly for six straight days. Worker and drone grubs are only fed it for three days. For the next three days, they eat a watery mixture of honey and pollen.

Looking after these white grubs is no easy task for the worker bees since each one has to be fed 1300 times a day.

A Rest Before Hatching

After their six-day feast, the grubs are sealed back into their nursery cells. Inside these cozy rooms they spin themselves cocoons and begin to change into adult bees.

The workers make sure the temperature of the hive is just right for the grubs. If the hive cools down, thousands of workers huddle together to warm it up. If it gets too warm, the workers sprinkle water on the cells and fan them with their wings.

In less than two weeks, the grubs become adult bees. They tear open their nursery cells and pop out, fully grown.

A worker's work is never done!

Bee of All Trades

Most of the hatching honeybees are females. They will become the worker bees of the hive and have many jobs—janitor, nurse, construction worker, security guard and food finder.

For the first three weeks, the new worker bees help out inside the hive. They clean cells, feed grubs, make wax for building and repairing the honeycombs or become guards at the hive entrances.

After about three weeks the young bees may leave the hive and search for food. They start by making short flights close to the hive until they learn how to find their way home from faraway fields.

Being a worker bee is such hard work that most of them look scruffy by the time they are four weeks old. Although the workers that are born in the fall usually live through the winter, spring and summer workers rarely live more than six weeks.

Opposite page:

The dandelion is a favorite honeybee feeding station.

Good to the Last Drop

How often have you poked your nose into a flower only to find yourself face to face with a bee? You only stopped for a sniff, but the bee was there for a tasty meal! Everything a bee needs to eat can be found inside a flower.

Try plucking a clover blossom and nibbling the base of its petals. What do you taste? Something very sweet? This sugary juice is called nectar. In some flowers the nectar is hard to reach. But the bee is well prepared for this. It has a built-in drinking straw called a proboscis. Just as you use a straw to slurp up those last delicious drops, a bee uses its proboscis to suck up the tiny nectar droplets.

A honeybee worker carries most of the nectar back to the hive in its stomach. Instead of having just one stomach like we do, a bee has two. It uses one stomach to digest some of the nectar for food. The rest goes into a special honey stomach to be taken back to the hive.

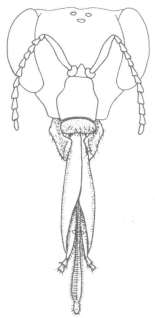

Honeybee proboscis

Opposite page:

In winter, when there are no flowers in the fields to provide nectar, honeybees live on honey, nature's liquid gold.

Honey Factory

As the workers are flying in the field they begin to turn the nectar they have gathered into honey. The nectar is pumped in and out of their honey stomach to remove some of the water in it. When they reach the hive, the field bees squirt this sweet liquid into a cell. Other bees work on the nectar to remove even more water. Finally, when the honey is ready, it is sealed in a wax storage cell.

Making honey is no easy task. Even though a bee's honey stomach is little bigger than a grain of rice, it may take as many as 1000 flower visits to fill it. To make just one thimbleful of honey, a single bee probably works ten hours a day for six days straight. That is hard work!

Hard at work making honey.

Pollen Baskets

The honeybee is one of nature's gardeners. Many flowers cannot use their own pollen to make seeds. They must get it from other flowers. But how, since they cannot move around?

Each time a bee visits a flower, some of the flower's powdery pollen gets caught in the hair on its body and legs. The bee spreads this pollen from flower to flower. Bees' work of spreading pollen is so important that some farmers put hives in orchards, fields and gardens so the bees and flowers are close together.

Pollen is also part of the bees' baby food. Using a built-in comb and brush on its legs, the bee collects the pollen from her hair and mouth parts. She carries it home to the hive in pollen baskets on her hind legs.

Her pollen baskets full, this honeybee will soon head for home.

Dance Directions

When you make an exciting discovery you use words to tell your friends about it. When a bee finds a new patch of sweet flowers it passes on the message to other bees in the hive by *dancing*. Honeybees have two dances—a round dance and a waggle. The bee does a round dance if the flowers are nearby and waggles for places farther away.

As the bee begins to dance, the other bees cluster around her to study her movements, smell the hairs on her body and taste the nectar she has collected. From these clues they will know what kind of flower to look for and where.

First those closest to the dancer join in the frenzied dance. Soon a long train of bees dances behind the leader to pass the message on. The new bees do not need to follow the dancer to the new flower patch. After they have been given the dance directions, they can make a beeline for the flowers all by themselves.

Silent Scent Signals

Bees have another way of communicating besides dancing. They send scent messages for other bees to smell. They use special scents to mark their hives and warn trespassers to stay out. The queen produces another scent to tell the drones when she is ready to mate. And if you have ever been stung by a bee, you were probably marked by a bee's scent message too. It warned other bees to be careful—YOU were dangerous!

The honeybee uses its stinger as a weapon to defend its colony.

Ouch!

Being stung by a bee will hurt you, and it will probably kill the bee. The bee's tiny stinger gets hooked so firmly in your skin that the bee tears its body when it tries to fly away. The bee will die after losing its stinger.

When it stings the bee leaves a tiny drop of venom under your skin. It is the venom that causes the puffy itchy red spot on your skin.

Some people think that bees sting because they are naturally bad tempered but this is not true. A bee will only sting if it is caught or hurt or if it feels that that the hive is in danger. The main danger comes from other animals that want to get at the sweet treat inside the hive.

Bears, skunks and even "robber" bees from other colonies will brave a stinging for a tasty honey lunch. To warn of an attack, the hive has guard bees. They stand at the hive entrances, and use their antennae to pick up any strange vibrations or odors. If the guards sense danger, they quickly pass the message through the hive and the counterattack begins.

Worker bee's stinger

Venom duct

Barbs

Opposite page:

Anytime you see a bee on a flower you can be sure it is a female since only the females work.

45

Honeybees Forever!

Honeybees will fight to protect their queen and their hive. They will even die to make sure their hive is safe.

Every honeybee in the hive has its own job to do. The queen lays her eggs so that there will always be bees to take care of the hive. In another part of the castlelike hive the drones wait for food and the next queen's mating flight. And the tireless little worker bees buzz endlessly in and out and around the hive. Out to the flowers they fly and back again to store the thick sweet food that has made them famous—honey. Mmm, mmm—long live the honeybee colonies of the world!

Words to Know

Antennae   A pair of sensitive feelers on the top of the bee's head.

Cocoon   The silky covering that a bee grub spins around itself.

Cells   Tiny six-sided wax rooms where young bees develop and honey and wax are stored.

Drone   A male bee.

Exoskeleton   The hard outer covering which forms a bee's body.

Grub   A baby bee.

Hive   A bee's home.

Honeycomb   Rows of wax cells in which honey is stored and the eggs are laid.

Nectar   A sweet juice that is made by flowers.

Pollen   A sticky powder that all flowers make and many exchange to make seeds.

Proboscis   A hollow tube like a drinking straw attached to a bee's mouth and used to suck up nectar.

Queen   The leader of a bee colony and the one who lays the eggs.

Royal jelly   A special baby food that the worker bees make and feed to the grubs.

Swarm   A large number of worker bees with a queen that have left their hive to start a new colony.

Venom   A poison that a bee leaves behind after stinging.

Workers   The female bees who build and guard the hive, look after the queen and gather food.

INDEX

Cover Photo: Robert C. Simpson (Valan Photos)
Photo Credits: Bill Ivy, pages 4, 8, 11, 12, 15, 16, 23, 28, 33, 34, 38, 40, 43, 44;
V. Claerhout, page 7; Treat Davidson (Miller Services), pages 19, 37; Harold
Lambert (Miller Services), page 24; Michel Bourque (Valan Photos), pages 27,
31. Illustration, pages 20-21 by Arabelle Wheatley, courtesy of *Encyclopedia
Americana*.

Printed and Bound in Italy by Lego SpA